Stile on Glyndwr's Way east of Llanidloes

GLYNDWR'S WAY

Mike Salter

FOLLY PUBLICATIONS

ACKNOWLEDGMENTS

The photographs and maps are all by Mike Salter. Thanks are due to the staff at Aspect Design for their help in assembling artwork of the book for publication, and to trail officer Helen Tatchell for help and advice.

AUTHOR'S NOTES

The whole of Glyndwr's Way was walked by the author in April and May 2012. Every effort has been made to ensure information is accurate and up-to-date at the time of publication but the author/publisher does not accept any responsibility for any accidents to users, nor is any responsibility accepted for any problems that might arise through any of the information given being inaccurate, incomplete or becoming out-of-date. Please take careful note of the suggestions about navigation and outdoor safety given on page 28.

Main distances are given in miles, still the most familiar unit of measurement for most British people. Distances are given from the starting point at Knighton. Shorter distances along the trail are estimated in yards. Heights are given in metres because modern Ordnance Survey maps are metric. The contours on Landranger maps are at 10m intervals, i.e. crossing three of them means climbing or descending roughly 100 feet. The terms used to describe the route are defined on page 28.

ABOUT THE AUTHOR

Mike Salter is 58 and has been a professional author and publisher since 1988. He is particularly interested in the planning and layout of medieval buildings and has a huge collection of plans of castles, abbeys and old churches measured during tours (mostly by bicycle and motorcycle) throughout all parts of the British Isles since 1968. Born and bred in Wolverhampton, Mike now lives in an old cottage beside the Malvern Hills. Since walking Land's End to John O'Groats in 2004 following his 50th birthday he has done many other long distance backpacking trails, averaging 1,000 miles a year. Mike is a life member of the YHA and English Heritage and he is also a member of the Mountain Bothies Association, the Backpackers Club, and the National Trust. His other interests include railways, board games, morris dancing of all kinds, and calling folk dances and playing percussion occasionally with ceilidh bands.

Abbey Cwmhir Church, capital from Cwmhir Abbey

Copyright 2012 Mike Salter
(t/a Folly Publications).
First published June 2012.
Folly Cottage,
151 West Malvern Road,
Malvern, Worcs, WR14 4AY.

Printed by Aspect Design
89 Newtown Road, Malvern,
Worcs WR14 2PD

Footbridge to the NW of Abbey Cwmhir

CONTENTS

ABOUT THE TRAIL

Glyndwr's Way was conceived and created by Powys County Council about the time of the Millennium and raised in status in 2002 as one of Britain's nineteen national trails. It is signposted with fingerboards at intervals. Between them gates and stiles and occasional marker posts usually bear three markings, the acorn symbol used on all national trails in England and Wales, the dragon symbol of Owain Glyndwr, and direction arrows combined with different colours to denote whether the next part of the trail is a path, bridleway, byway or road. Existing rights of way across farmland have been used to create the trail, only small sections of which cross commonland or open moor. There are also short sections through forest.

Note that because the trail lies entirely within Powys it does not visit all of the places associated with Owain Glyndwr. His estates of Sycharth and Glyndyfyrwy lie on the southern fringes of Denbighshire 20 miles NE of any part of Glyndwr's Way, whilst the castle of Harlech where he held court for several years lies considerably round the Merionedd coast from Machynlleth.

The trail route has been very considerably altered over the last ten years mainly to eliminate the long sections of road originally used. Currently about a fifth of the 132 mile long trail is on tarmac surfaces, half these sections being along dead-end farm lanes not carrying through traffic, and none of the tarmac sections are longer than 2 miles. That's about as much off-road walking as is possible for a trail in England and Wales. There has also been a trend towards altering rights of way along the trail so as to now go round the side of each farm rather than though the middle of the farmyard itself. A result of these changes, which are still ongoing, is that no set of Ordnance Survey maps shows the exact current route of each and every part of the trail.

There is wonderful scenery along the whole of Glyndwr's Way, and, mainly because there are hardly any level sections of more than a mile or two, the views tend to change quite quickly. The downside of this is the very large amount of climbing to be done. In total there is about 6500 metres (20,000 feet) of ascent along the trail. Most people walk the trail over about nine days. Anyone completing Glyndwr's Way within a week will have climbed the equivalent of ascending a 900 metre (3,000 feet) high mountain each day.

Trains offer the best access to Glyndwr's Way. Machynlleth and Welshpool are linked by trains about every two hours to Shrewsbury and Birmingham, each of which offers varied connections to other places. Knighton has just four trains each way between Shrewsbury, Craven Arms, Llandrindod Wells, Llanelli and Swansea. Knighton also has buses connecting it with Leominster and Ludlow (for trains to and from Hereford) but note that these are infrequent.

Glyndwr's Way is roughly horseshoe-shaped but it can be made into a full circuit of about 160 miles by using the Severn Way along a canal towpath northwards for 3 miles from Welshpool and then south for 25 miles along Offa's Dyke path from Buttington back to Knighton. Another possibility for a walk of about 130 miles is to use the Ceredigion Coast Path from Cardigan to Machynlleth and then the second half of Glyndwr's Way to go through to Welshpool.

It is legal to take a dog along Glyndwr's Way provided it is on a lead at all times. In practice sheep farmers will not be pleased to see your dog on their lands at lambing time however well controlled. If you must take a dog why not go later in the year when lambing and ground nesting birds are less likely to be disturbed by your dog even if it is on a lead. The trend is for replacing stiles on the trail by special new pedestrian width gates. Where stiles do exist they are sometimes accompanied by special dog gates with vertical sliding doors.

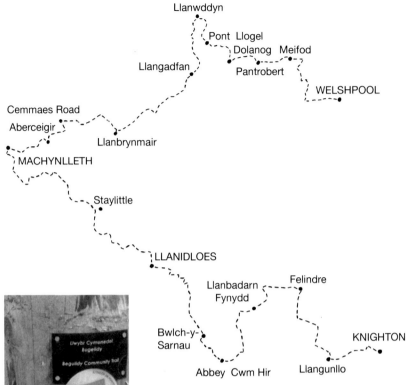

Trail markers on Glyndwr's Way

Those using B&B type accommodation will need to book well in advance and to be able to cover up to 16 miles of strenuous walking in a day. No youth hostels lie anywhere near Glyndwr's Way but there are two bunkhouses. Between the starting point in the town of Knighton and the finishing point in the town of Welshpool the only major supply points are the towns of Llanidloes and Machynlleth 46 and 74 miles along the trail respectively. The second half of the trail beyond Machynlleth has more intermediate village shops, pubs, cafes and public toilets, plus craft shops at Llanwddyn.

Only ten places along the trail have official camp sites, leaving gaps of up to 24 miles between them. Because so much of the trail is on farm land wild camping is only possible in a few remote places. It is legal to stop for rest or refreshment whilst walking along a right-of-way but there is no right to erect any sort of shelter. Ask permission from farmers if in doubt. Be discreet at all times if you do wild camp. Pitch fairly late in the day well out of sight from roads and dwellings and use a tent with a flysheet of a colour that blends in with the surroundings. Don't light fires, leave rubbish or loiter in large groups. Bear in mind farmers usually check on their sheep late at night and early in the morning. They may be friendly but their dogs might cause you problems. Most of the streams you will be crossing have flowed over fields where animals graze so don't drink the water without either boiling it or treating it with tablets first.

OWAIN GLYNDWR - A BRIEF HISTORY

Owain Glyndwr is a folk hero for the Welsh, being the last Welshman to use the title of Prince of Wales. He claimed descendancy from the princes of Deheubarth from his mother Elen ferch Tomas ap Llywelyn, and from the princes of Powys through his father Gruffydd Fychan, who died when Owain was a child. Heir to the Denbighshire estates of Sycharth and Glyndyfrdwy, he may have been brought up in the household of David Hanmer, whose daughter he married in 1383 after legal training in London. During the next two years Owain did garrison duty at Berwick-upon-Tweed and was on campaign in Scotland with John of Gaunt, Duke of Lancaster. In 1387 Owain served under Richard Fitz-Alan, Earl of Arundel in a naval battle against the French off the Kent coast and also fought under Gaunt's son the future Henry IV at Radcot Bridge in Oxfordshire where Richard II's favourite the Earl of Oxford was defeated.

In the 1390s Owain settled down to life as a gentleman living in an elaborate timber-framed mansion within the old 12th century earthwork castle at Sycharth. There he was visited by the bard Iolo Goch, whose poetry praised Owen's liberality and saying how rare it was to see anything hidden away behind a latch or lock at Sycharth. A powerful neighbour, Reginald, Lord de Grey of Ruthin, claimed lands Owain considered his. De Grey also held back a summons to Owain for service with the royal forces in Scotland. Owain took de Grey to court in 1400 but the result was a forgone conclusion because de Grey was an ally of the newly crowned Henry VI, who had recently deposed and murdered Richard II. In September 1400 Owain was driven to open rebellion, proclaiming himself Prince of Wales. After some early successes by Owain the revolt was nearly stamped out by Henry IV's vigorous campaigning Wales.

However, because of the circumstances of his accession, Henry IV's position was non too secure. There were many powerful people that were either against him or whom he couldn't trust. Penal laws passed against the Welsh in 1402 only served to increase support for Owain. It was a good year for Owain. He surprised and captured Reginald de Grey, who was only released many months later after Henry IV agreed to pay a huge ransom. The king refused to ransom another of Owain's prisoners, Sir Edmund Mortimer, who had been defeated and captured at the battle of Pilleth, near Knighton. Mortimer and his young nephew Edmund each had a better claim to the throne than Henry IV and Mortimer agreed to change sides and marry one of Owain's daughters.

In 1403 the powerful Percy family holding the earldoms of Northumberland and Worcester fell out with Henry IV. A bold plan was drawn up for the king's overthrow with the Percies to rule all of northern England, the Mortimers southern England and Owain Glyndwr getting Wales and parts of England west of the River Severn. In the summer of 1403 the impulsive Hotspur Percy brought an army down to the Marches but failed to meet up with the forces of Glyndwr, who probably didn't get to hear of Hotspur's plans in time and was busy campaigning in Carmarthenshire. The battle of Shrewsbury that resulted was a very narrow victory for Henry IV. His army suffered very heavy casualties and his son Prince Henry was severely disfigured by an arrow wound in the face. However, Hotspur also got hit in the head by an arrow and was instantly killed.

Early in 1404 the castle of Harlech was surrendered to Owain after being blockaded since 1401. Glyndwr took Harlech as his chief residence and held a Welsh parliament (cyholliad - gathering) at Machynlleth to set up a government for an independent Wales using the laws of Hywell Dda and with a plan for a university in each of the north and south parts of Wales. Welsh students at Oxford had given up their studies to return to Wales to join Owain's forces.

The castle of Aberystwyth which had been surrendered to Glyndwr's forces in 1404 after a very long blockade and the capture of its supply ship, was blockaded by Prince Henry during 1406 and eventually retaken a year later after a close siege using cannon. By then the tide had turned against Owain Glyndwr and French and Breton forces sent over to help him had returned home. Of Edward I's five major new castles built in the 1280s and 90s to encircle Gwynedd only Caernarfon and Beaumaris had never been captured by Glyndwr's forces, Conwy having fallen to the Tudor brothers through a stratagem.

An even more severe blow to Glyndwr was the recapture of Harlech by the English in 1409. His son-in-law Sir Edmund Mortimer died in the castle during the siege and Owain's wife Margaret and two of her daughters and several grandchildren were captured and taken off to the Tower of London where they all died after a few years. His son Gruffudd, captured in a separate campaign, also died in an English prison c1412. Owain himself was last heard of in that year, when he made several successful raids and captured Dafydd Gam at Brecon. Glyndwr was probably then in his early or mid 50s (his date of birth is unknown). He had continually and actively defied the English Crown for twelve years, half of a generation, something no Welsh lord (or English lord either) had ever managed to achieve. Just over seventy years later another Welshman, Henry Tudor, Earl of Richmond would defeat Richard III and take the English throne as Henry VII, from whom our present royal family are descended.

Much of the Owain Glyndwr enigma stems from the fact that no-one knows for sure what happened to him after 1412, which gave rise to the myth that he would appear again when the Welsh needed him to free them of English oppression. Prince Henry succeeded his father as King Henry V in 1413 and offered Owain Glyndwr a pardon in the hope that achieving peace in Wales would help his more glamorous ambitions to recover crown possessions lost in France. Owain never replied to that offer. It says a lot that no-one ever betrayed him. In 1414 rumours circulated that Glyndwr had died, possibly an attempt to cover his tracks, whilst Adam of Usk's chronicle records his death and secret burial in 1415. Three of Owain's daughters had married into Herefordshire landed families, the Crofts, the Monningtons and the Scudamores. A popular story has it that Alice and her husband Sir John Scudamore of Kentchurch Court (which lies just south of the road between Abergavenny and Hereford) kept Owain in disguise (without his beard) as their parish priest known as Jack of Kent for a few years until he died of natural causes. Through his daughter Alice Owain Glyndwr's blood line is said to live on through such noted families as the de Vere earls of Oxford and the Cavendish dukes of Devonshire.

A Welsh character called Owen Glendower appears in the Shakespeare play Henry IV part I. The play perpetuates the idea of Owain Glyndwr's supposed mystic powers, who can "call sprits from the vasty deep". Glyndwr's popularity as a folk hero was rekindled by romantic writers in the 19th century and in the early 20th century the Welsh prime minister David Lloyd George unveiled a statue of him in Cardiff Civic Hall. In 2000 a memorial to Owain Glyndwr was put up in Machynlleth to celebrate 600 years since he first rebelled against unjust English rule in Wales and proclaimed himself as Prince of Wales.

For further information about Owain Glyndwr's life and times see Owen Glendower by J.E.Lloyd, 1931, and The Revolt of Owain Glyn Dwr by R. Rees Davies, 1995. Attacks by Glyndwr's forces against castles and abbeys in Wales are recorded in several of Mike Salter's books (see list inside back of cover).

ROUTE DESCRIPTION

KNIGHTON

Knighton is a small town of 3000 people set on the eastern edge of the former county of Radnor created in 1536, now the central part of Powys. A small part of the town beyond the north bank of the River Teme, including the fine Victorian railway station of 1865, is actually in England, forming part of the Shropshire parish of Stowe. Knighton's Welsh name Tref-y-Clawydd means Town on the Dyke, referring to Offa's Dyke, which is visible on the hillsides north and south of the town with the Offa's Dyke National Trail closely following it. This trail enters the town from the south via Broad Street and leaves via a park to the NE, where there is a commemorative stone. Traces of the dyke survive there. In the medieval period the dyke formed part of the vanished town defences, which were probably of earth and wood rather than a wall of stone. The town was garrisoned by the Mortimers against Owain Glyndwr in 1402.

The town has a fair range of shops, services and places to stay, plus occasional trains and buses. There are public toilets in a car-park on the south side of Broad Street but only hot water is available there. Cold water can be obtained from a tap hidden under a grey box beside the tower of the parish church of St Edward reached by walking down Church Street from the central Clock Tower of 1872. The church tower is 14th century with a recessed pyramidal-roofed bellstage of timber, a common type along the Welsh border. Otherwise the church is of little interest, having been rebuilt in 1875-7.

Old house in Knighton

The Clock Tower marks where Glyndwr's Way leaves Offa's Dyke Path. A sign points up the steep and appropriately named Narrows, where a Glyndwr's Way stone and information board will be found. Carry on up to a T-junction. The trail turns left here and bends right down a narrow lane which soon opens out on the left to give southward views across a steep-sided valley. Hidden behind buildings on the right, set on the highest point of the town, is the motte of a late 11th century castle (go right at the T-junction and keep left to eventually get a view of it and carry on to join the official trail further along). This castle was stormed and captured by the Welsh in 1215 and Knighton then remained in Welsh hands until 1230, when it became part of the dowry of Llywelyn ab Iorwerth's daughter on her marriage to Ralph Mortimer. Possibly then rebuilt in stone, this castle was finally destroyed by Llywelyn ap Gruffydd in 1262. By the playing fields east of the town is a second castle mound, Bryn Castell, possibly the site of a castle built by Brian Brampton during the period when the town and the other castle were in Welsh hands.

The lane past the castle site is followed for 500 yards before it drops down and opens out. Take the footpath signed up to the right and climb up, crossing firstly the driveway of a house and then the B4355. Continue to climb on a path to the left of new houses. At the top go right on a road for a short distance and then fork left through a gate onto a path through woodland, having now left the new houses behind and soon getting a view down to the right of the town centre below. Apart from small villages offering minimal services nothing but hilly open country now lies ahead of you for the next 45 miles to Llanidloes.

Marker at start of trail in Knighton

There is nearly a mile of woodland path before you turn left onto a road. Shortly turn left onto another road which drops down, passing a seat where a lane goes off to the left, and another seat further down, shortly after which turn right on a farm lane which eventually turns into a track as it climbs 140 metres. Go through a gate into a field and follow the right-hand hedge. Keep left of a small pond in the next field and go up to join a track, turning left along it. Keep to the left-hand fence after entering a field and after a gate drop down slightly. By a new sign saying Knighton 4.25 miles and Llangunllo 2.25 miles join a more obvious track leading down. After 300 yards go left on a path across a field to cross a stream and then follow a track for 120 yards before leaving it to drop down to the right to recross the stream. Go through a gate and follow the left-hand hedge to reach a track going down for 100 yards. At a junction of tracks go straight over into what looks like a private garden. After a few yards you will find an information board about the farm here, Cefn-suran, and a path forking slightly right through a short belt of woodland. Go left onto a track and pass through a gate. Go right and head WNW through fields to reach a lane. Go down it left a few yards and then through a gate to drop down on a path through woods on the right. Cross over a farm track and descend to B4356. Go right to find the centre of the village of Llangunllo, 6.5miles from Knighton.

A path left of a white house gives access to the churchyard of the church of St Cynllo where you can shelter in the porch of 1896. The church was rebuilt in 1878 and the embattled west tower is of 1894 so the only old parts are a reset doorway and one north-facing lancet window. The village has a pub by the main road-junction but offers no other services to walkers/backpackers.

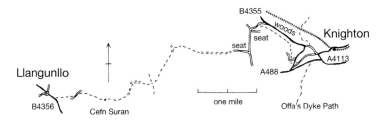

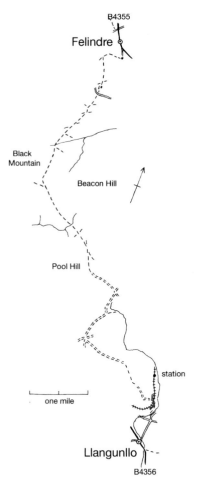

From the road junction at Llangunllo take the lane heading north. Shortly after crossing over another road after a third of a mile go left on a path leading down to a bridge over a stream. Climb back up and go right on a lane to pass under the railway. Keep on the lane along the west side of the railway for 400 yards if you need the station, otherwise immediately after the railway bridge take a track off left heading west to start with, but later going NW as it climbs. After half a mile the track leads to a path still heading NW. Eventually, after following a field boundary which is kept to your right, this leads to a level section of green lane two thirds of a mile long. At the end go right and over a crossroads of tracks at the Ordnance Survey spot height of 367 metres and climb quite steeply for half a mile. Just over three miles from Llangunllo you will pass though a short section of forest and arrive at a junction of tracks at about the 470 metre contour. A sign proclaims the large expanse of open moor here as the Crown lands of Cytir Beacon Hill and that birds likely to be spotted include the meadow pipit, skylark, whinchat, buzzard, peregrine and wheatear, while occasional visitors in wetter years might include the curlew, snape and ring ouzel.

Go left at the crossing of tracks, initially with forest on your left. There is a good track for two thirds of a mile to the WNW, then a fainter track continues heading NNW, passing just to the right of the top of Pool Hill, home of the rare pillwort. The bridleway dips slightly into the very top of Cwm Dwliwnt, climbs to pass just to the right of the summit of Stanky Hill and drops to a saddle. The good track then carries on left down the valley but Glyndwr's Way goes off on what is initially a fainter track which soon bends right to go northwards over the east end of Black Mountain. Drop down to a muddy stream crossing and then carry on up NNE to go over Warren Bank. The final ridge to go over is Cefn Pawl. Here you cross over an unfenced road and head left to go round the left or west side of the farm. Briefly join a track then go left to descend on a bridleway. On reaching woodland turn right onto a bridleway which soon leads to a track which descends steeply heading east. Turn left at Brandy House Farm (which offers camping and accommodation) to go down the farm lane to join B4355. A second campsite lies in the village, which lies 16m from Knighton, but the shop has closed down and the pub only opens in the evenings. There is a bus shelter for a very occasional bus service along the B4355.

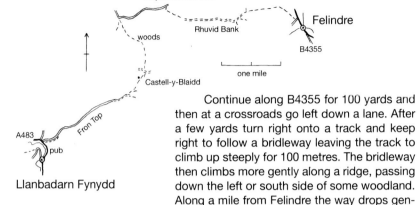

Continue along B4355 for 100 yards and then at a crossroads go left down a lane. After a few yards turn right onto a track and keep right to follow a bridleway leaving the track to climb up steeply for 100 metres. The bridleway then climbs more gently along a ridge, passing down the left or south side of some woodland. Along a mile from Felindre the way drops gently and bends right then left to pass through the farmyard of Rhuvid. Follow a track westwards up onto another ridge, Rhuvid Bank. This turns into a bridleway following a field boundary. At a gate go right briefly almost up to Hope's Castle Farm before doing a hairpin turn to go left, heading west down the tarmac farm lane (the sign at the sharp bend is easy to miss)). Gradually descend for nearly a mile.

When the lane goes right you go left and drop slightly to cross a bridge before following a path over rough ground back up and through woodland. Go over a hump and look slightly right to see a bridge to cross. Then head south and cross over a track. Near the crossing humps and bumps of ancient farmsteads can be seen. Rise up to a post at a field boundary corner and keep right, going between it and Castell-y-Blaidd, about which nothing is known either historically or archeologically, but it is assumed to be a 12th century ringwork. Heading SW, climb up onto the ridge beyond the earthwork and go right onto a track which eventually becomes a lane. Glyndwr's Way stays on the lane all the way down to A483, except for a path going through three fields on the left or south of the lane at the bottom end, although two very muddy gateways hardly make this path worth using. Follow a pavement alongside A4832 heading south for nearly half a mile, passing a pub with a garden with a waterfall as a backdrop. The way turns right down a lane to a display board but you can take a slight short cut to the board by going through the churchyard of St Padarn's Church at Llanbadarn Fynydd, which lies 23m from Knighton. Although much restored in 1894 the church has one 14th century north window and a roof of c1500. The head beam of the rood screen also survives. By the porch are loose capitals from Abbey Cwm Hir which is your next port of call.

Castell y Blaidd (Castle of the Wolf)

From the signboard and church at Llanbadarn Fynydd cross over the river Ithon and carry on northwards along the lane for 150 yards climbing slightly. After the hairpin bend go right onto a track climbing steeply at first. This continues as a bridleway across fields, keeping close to the left hand or southern boundary. Just before reaching a small clump of trees turn left at a crossing of bridleways and head SSW on the level to another junction, where you fork left to go over a new bridge and climb heading SSE over the west flank of Moel Dod guided by occasional posts. Pass right of a strip of trees and continue SSW and then SSE along the ridge. There's a short climb after crossing a stream. Pass along a strip of trees and then descend down gently towards a house. Look left at this point to see Castell Tinboeth on the other side of the valley in which lies A483. This was a mid to late 13th century stronghold of the Mortimers, probably short-lived and likely to have been built to replace Castell-y-Blaidd which you have already passed. The one low stonework fragment visible is thought to have formed part of a twin-towered gatehouse facing NE.

In front of the house you have dropped towards go left to descend more steeply eastwards down a track which bends round to pass through the farmyard of Tynypant. At the saddle cross over the lane onto another farm lane, which is used for 100 yards before you fork right and climb up, following a row of trees to start, onto another high ridge. Pass not far to the left or east of a triangulation point elevated at 440 metres. Continue on the obvious bridleway heading SE for another 500 yards. At a crossing turn sharp right to descend just beneath where you have just come along for 100 yards and then descend steeply to a gate taking the bridleway down beside a stream through a forest.

Go left at the bottom to join the lane serving a farm to your right. A short loop of path with a footbridge over the Bachell Brook offers an alternative to negotiating the cattle grid on the lane. Climb to a road and go left for a mile of up and down following the brook. Just before the lane passes Richard Fowler's house of Dyfaenor of c1670 Glyndwr's Way goes up steps to the right and crosses a field through to a woodland path. Cross a stream, climb back up past a house and go into a field. Stay close to the right-hand boundary and go through a gate in it to pass another house to your left, ie south or below you. Enter forest and join the drive of the second house to a road. Take the left fork as the road divides and this leads you down into the delightful village of Abbey Cwm Hir, passing on the left on the way in the abbey ruins, then a farmyard with a display about the abbey in one of the buildings, and then arriving at the church and pub, which lie 31 miles from Knighton.

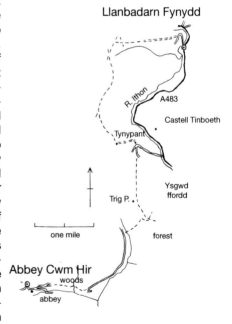

Llanbadarn Fynydd

R. Ithon

A483

Castell Tinboeth

Tynypant

Trig P.

Ysgwd ffordd

one mile

forest

Abbey Cwm Hir

woods

abbey

The scanty remains of the church of Cwm Hir Abbey

Cwm Hir Abbey was originally founded in 1143 but was refounded in 1176 with monks from Whitland. It then prospered and huge new church on a larger scale than any of the four medieval Welsh cathedrals was begun in the 1190s and continued into the 1220s under patronage from Llywelyn ab Iorwerth. Here in 1282 was buried his grandson Llywelyn ap Gruffydd, the last Welsh ruler to call himself Prince of Wales before Owain Glyndwr claimed that title. Work on the buildings may have stopped in 1231 when the abbey was threatened with destruction by Henry III of England after part of his army was lured into a trap by one of the monks. Latterly the abbey fell on hard times and when suppressed by Henry VIII's officials in 1536 its lands were worth just £28 per annum. The site is typical of those favoured by Cistercian monks, a remote valley where they could divide their time between quiet contemplation and the hard work involved in cultivation and large scale sheep farming. The valley here hardly seems wide enough for a full layout of claustral buildings. All we have left of the buildings are bare outlines of the outer walls of a huge fourteen bay aisled nave of the church. Low parts of the west walls of transepts also survive but it is uncertain whether the rest of the eastern part of the church was ever completed. Part of one of the arcades has been erected in the parish church at Llanidloes. The church doorway at Llanfair Caereinion is also probably from the abbey. You will have already seen loose capitals from the abbey at Llanbadarn Fynydd and you will find others probably from the arcades between the alleys and garth of the cloister beside the parish church of St Mary here. The church itself is of 1866 but has a relief of the Ascension over the porch doorway cop-ied from a tympanum found at the abbey. There is also the lid of the coffin of Abbot Mabli, c1200. The pub opposite the church is called the Happy Union and has in one of its buildings a post office with a few food items on sale.

From the new signpost beside an old petrol pump just west of the entrance to the churchyard go north on a short length of lane leading to a track into a forest. Climb up to a saddle then drop down passing another forest track high up and another further down. Carry on down to a bridge over the Clywedog Brook and climb up to join a road. A recent diversion now has the way following this road slightly uphill northwards for half a mile before turning left onto a track climbing up to Esgair. Keep on the track until signed off right into a field to bypass a farmyard. Rejoin the track to continue climbing onto a ridge. Go through a gate to the right and then through another gate and keep fairly close to the fence on your left. Pass to the left of a clump of trees and turn right onto a rutted farm track leading down into the village of Bwlch-y-Sarnau lying just over 34m from Knighton. It offers no services to walkers/backpackers.

Go left up a road and turn left beside the chapel. Almost immediately a track leads down to the right into a farmyard. Continue heading NW on a footpath. Follow the stream and cross it and enter a forest on a path. After two thirds of a mile on the level join a track to keep going in the same direction to a road. Go left and then immediately right on another road which is followed for almost a mile past Waun and through a forest. At the point where Glyndwr's Way goes off on a track to the right there is a gateway onto another track going more back to the right and here there are stones to sit on for a break. Follow the track almost on the level for over a mile. After a dropping to cross a valley the track becomes a farm lane for 300 yards to a new sign saying Abbey Cwm Hir 6.75 miles and Llanidloes 8.5 miles.

By the signpost go right on a track which drops into a valley with signs of quarrying. The way then follows a bridleway for 500 yards to a track. Go left to drop down onto a farm lane. Turn right to climb back up to a farm. After climbing for another 100 yards go left then immediately right (almost a crossroads) on a track for 600 yards passing an old farmhouse now just used as a barn. Climb up and turn left at a crossing of tracks. After a short while descend very steeply to a stream. Turn left along a path to a bridge and then climb up steeply on a path beside the stream. Go over a stile and climb up steeply through a field to a stile onto a track. Go left and continue up for 300 yards. Turn right onto a farm lane and carry on climbing. Go straight ahead on a track and then descend on a path through a field and then turn left on a rough path following the contour but hardly level. Pass a twee isolated house and arrive at a track to climb up to the left to a saddle. Follow the bridleway leaving to the right and cross over a track and go through marshland. Go through a gate and rise up through two fields keeping close to the right-hand fence. Turn left to keep close to a another fence and cross over a track near the farm of Iaen-y-Cwm.

Go down through a field and turn right to reach a bridge in a steep little valley. Climb up and turn right onto a lane opposite a house. After 400 yards go right onto a road for 350 yards. By a chapel at Newchapel turn left onto a lane for 300 yards. Go left on a path to pass a house and across a field down to another footbridge in a steeply-sided wooded valley. Climb back up and carry on up on a path in a side-valley to a lane which drops down to the west, following a stream. At the edge of Llanidloes the lane bends left. After a few yards a path on the right leads under A470 and through towards the middle of the town of Llanidloes, which lies 46 miles from Knighton via Glyndwr's Way.

Llanidloes

A470

one mile

Newchapel

Moelfre

forest

Waun

Bwlch-y-sarnau

Esgair

forest

Abbey Cwm Hir

Llanidloes Town Hall

Established in the 1280s by Owain de la Pole, Lord of Powys, and a borough until 1974, Llanidloes is a town of 2300 people beside the River Severn. The Health Centre and Community Centre in Mount Street lie on the site of a wooden castle. The town offers a fair range of shops and services, plus a few buses connecting it with railway stations at Caersws, Newtown, Welshpool and Shrewsbury. Llanidloes lost its own railway in 1962. There were once lead and silver mines nearby and the town produced flannel. It has always been a quirky independent place. There were Chartist riots here in 1839. Local hippies, of which there are many, have started up an annual green fair. At the central cross-roads is the half-timbered market hall of c1600, the only one of its type left in Wales, once used for assize courts and the scene in 1748 of preaching by John Wesley. The church of St Idloes has a late 14th century west tower. The magnificent hammerbeam roof dates from 1542 when the church was much enlarged by adding a north aisle with a five bay arcade of re-used 13th century piers and arches from Cwm Hir Abbey, which was also the source of the south doorway.

From the Town Hall in the middle of Llanidloes head north on Long Bridge Street and go left at a roundabout to cross the River Severn on a three-arched bridge of 1826. Go left to climb up NW on B4518 for 150 yards before finding at the end of the houses a path up to the right into a forest. Go straight up for half a mile and then fork up left on a more minor path. After going north for 100 yards it bends left to head west out of the forest to a lane. Go a few yards to the right down the lane, then take a path dropping down on the left for 300 yards to a road. Cross over onto a track and after 100 yards go right up a bank. This leads through to a track which bends left to climb round the side of a hill and continues on the ridge as a path. Cross over a bridleway and after a short while the path is directed off left to keep clear of a house. It rises to join the drive of the house which leads back to B4518.

Go along the main road for 200 yards and then turn left onto a path which initially runs beside and above the main road. After 400 yards join a track down towards Bryntail which is bypassed to the north by a permissive path leaving the right-hand side of the track and rejoining it later. The track then bends right and descends towards the Clywedog Dam. Turn left and drop steeply to the ruins of Bryntail Lead Mine, where there is a footbridge across the Afon Clywedog. Climb up on a lane and go right to climb steeply on a winding road up towards the head of the dam, which is 51 miles from Knighton.

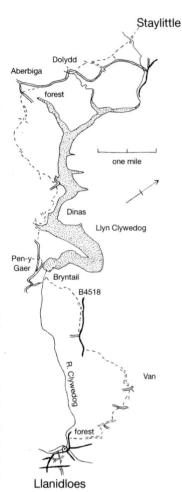

Staylittle
Dolydd
Aberbiga
forest
one mile
Dinas
Llyn Clywedog
Pen-y-Gaer
Bryntail
B4518
R. Clywedog
Van
forest
Llanidloes

Ruins of the Bryntail Lead Mine below the Clywedog Dam

Looking down on Llyn Clywedog from Pen-y-Gaer

The 240 yard long Clywedog Dam was completed in 1967 mainly to regulate the flow of water in the upper reaches of the River Severn to help prevent flooding but also to supply water to places as far away as Bristol. The dam is made of a series of hollow buttresses with overflows between them. The narrow and winding reservoir behind it is over 5 miles long. The hills here are rich in ancient hillforts. Just above the road above the SW end of the dam is Pen-y-Gaer, one of three hillforts in Montgomeryshire which had stone ramparts, now reduced to a spread of rubble. A gateway can be traced on the south side. The unfinished earthwork on the headland of Dinas just over a mile to the north on the other side of the reservoir is said to have been the location of the last stand of Caractacus against the Romans.

From just beyond the viewing platform above the dam a path climbs up steeply to an upper road. After the road bends left go right onto a path down to the shore of the reservoir. Go round an inlet and past a sailing club and then turn off the drive to the club-house to continue on a path keeping above the shoreline. Eventually you'll descend to the road. Cross over on a bridleway that gradually climbs above a side-valley for half a mile before going through a corner of a forest. Pass along the northern edge of the forest to a house and then go through a belt of forest to a saddle. Emerge on open ground and drop down to join a track leading back down to the road. Just as the road enters a forest go right on a path which zigzags and climbs to cut a corner of back up to the road. Follow the road for half a mile to Dolydd, and keep on the road as it goes over a bridge and swings to the right. After 100 yards Glyndwr's Way now goes off to the left on a track up to Nant-yr-Hafod, but stay on the road for just over another mile if you need accommodation or the shop in the village of Staylittle on B4518. The village is an old settlement serving travellers on the drove road between Machynlleth and Llanidloes and was on the original route taken by Glyndwr's Way.

Glyndwr's Way bypasses the farm of Nant-yr-Hafod by turning off left to climb above and behind it. Keep at the foot of the slope of Y Ffridd, going NNE on a path through fields. Cross over a track (which allows another escape route to the road to Staylittle) and go below a farm. Then head north through to a track. Turn left and cross a bridge over Afon Clywedog, then climb up steeply on a path up Rhiw Dyfeity Fawr. After a gate it is not clear where to go. Keep slightly right and join a track to head WNW over a ridge. If you go too far left you'll strike a new farm track first not on the maps and it leads you no-where. The correct track eventually bends westwards and passes an earthwork said to be a Roman fortlet. Drop into the saddle beyond and go left on a track for a short distance before taking a bridleway to the right leading over part of the ridge of Y Grug before dropping down the SW corner of the hill to a bridge by a corner of a forest. Climb back up onto a track. The easy option is to follow the track for two thirds of a mile and then turn right on another track passing the east end of Glaslyn. The right of way and with it Glyndwr's Way firstly does a loop west of the track and then cuts a corner off, but at the expense of going through bog to join the track heading north to the east of Glaslyn.

Go north on the track for half a mile and then fork off left on a track passing just below (south) of the summit of Foel Fadian. This is the highest point of the way, just over the 500 metre contour. After dropping steeply for 200 yards turn off left on a bridleway and after crossing a stream drop very steeply for half a mile. Join a track heading in the same direction above the stream. After a farm drop into the valley on a lane and climb up the other side. Fork right to carry on climbing up for 300 yards and then turn left on a bridleway. Turn off left on a path after 250 yards and drop down to a lane heading NW along the north side of Afon Dulas.

Go just past where a lane and a tributary stream come in from the left before turning left over a bridge and up the farm lane to Cleiriau. Carry on up on a track, bend left and hug the contour to go though a belt of forest. Go right at Talbontdrain and then go left of a house where a short-cut alternative is signed off right through it's yard. The long way climbs up to become a track which crosses a stream and goes into forest. Turn right and climb on steep rough ground up to a forest track. Just over two miles south of here lies Hyddgen, site of a battle in 1402 where Owain Glyndwr's archers defeated a larger English force which tried to attack their encampment.

Turn right onto the track and descend slightly to a crossing of tracks at a saddle. Go over to climb slightly beside forest but then keep left on a level bridleway firstly on the side of the steep slope and then on undulating ground. After a mile and a half from the crossing of tracks turn right at a T-junction of tracks. Drop slightly but then go left on a bridleway climbing back up to enter a recently harvested forest on a track which bends left after nearly a mile above Llyn Glanmerin. After leaving the forest fork left on a path to head west. The path drops and does a sharp bend to the right to head north before resuming a westerly course. Beyond Brynglas the way becomes a track dropping to a lane. Turn right to go through a saddle and then drop down on a path to the right with Machynlleth clearly visible ahead. Just as the path reaches A487 a road goes off right into parkland. This provides a back route for Glyndwr's Way to arrive in the centre of Machynlleth opposite the Parliament House associated with Owain Glyndwr's Welsh parliament of 1404, although actually slightly later in date. It lies 74 miles from Knighton.

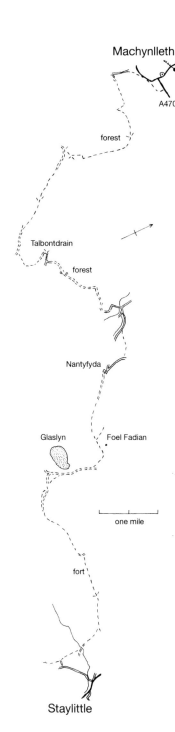

The Parliament House at Machynlleth

Machynlleth is a small town of about 2500 people and has a reasonable range of shops and services. It has always been a place of greater importance than its size and once had no fewer than 24 inns, the old bridge carrying A487 over the Dovey being the lowest crossing point of that river. This road, called Doll Street from a toll house on one side of it, passes the railway station and before that the parish church of St Peter with a 15th century west tower remodelled in the 18th century and a main body of 1827 re-placing the cruciform 13th century building. The Parliament House lies in Maen Gwyn Street, named after an old signpost set into a house wall. There was once another toll house on this street.

Side streets with the names of Garrisonj(Gariswn) and Barracks recall when Parliamentary forces had to be kept here to maintain the peace after the second Civil War of 1649 following the execution of King Charles I. At the T-shaped junction of the three main roads is a clock tower of 1873 built by the Marquess of Londonderry, whose family had inherited Plas Machynlleth from the Edwardes family. Now owned by the town council, and once called Greenfield, the house has 19th century facades grafted onto a 16th and 17th century core and hous-es an exhibition. Near the clock tower is a medieval house called Royal House, having supposedly been visited by Henry Tudor on his way to victory at Bosworth.

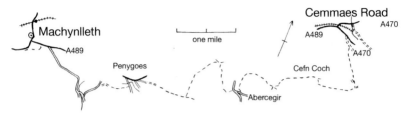

Glyndwr's way leaves Machynlleth by following A489 eastwards for 200 yards until a minor road forks off to the right. This is followed for almost a mile until Forge. After the bridge over Afon Dulas turn left on another road skirting round the NW flank of Is-y-coed for 400 yards. Turn right on what starts as a track but becomes a path along the north side of the hill. The way passes a house and joins its approach track. Go left onto a lane to cross Afon Crewi and reach A489 at Penycoes. Go right along A489 and take the second of two roads close together that fork off to the right. It becomes a track and then a bridleway heading east up towards Ffridd Wyllt. After reaching the end of the woods on the right, nearly a mile up from the main road, turn left going north on another bridleway which rises up to cross over a SW spur of Bryn Wg. On reaching some woods go right at a junction of bridleways to firstly go level NE and then uphill SE around a northern spur of Bryn Wg. Drop down to meet a track and cross over Nant Gwydol on a footbridge. Then climb up steps to a road at Abercegir, which is 5 miles from Machynlleth and 3.75 miles from Cemmaes Road according to a new sign post.

At Abercegir go left along the road for 80 yards and then back on yourself uphill to the right on another lane, passing some seats on the left. After 60 yards again go back on yourself, this time to the left, uphill on a path. After 80 yards go left into a field to skirt round the left side of a house. Shortly afterwards, when faced with a sign having a gate left of it an an opening to the right, take the opening and keep to the left-hand field boundary, gradually climbing round the west side of Rhos y Silio. After a while leave the wall and follow a feint track up onto the ridge After passing a saddle keep left of the next bit of the ridge summit but eventually swing right and then left again, keeping to the left or northern side of the ridge of Cefn Coch and above (to right of) the farm of Cefncoch gwyllt. Descend eastwards off the end of the ridge and go left on a track heading down NW. After a short way go right through a gate and cross fields descending NNW above the track you have just left. At the bottom go left onto a track to reach A470. Go left initially on a verge and then on a pavement beside the main road to the roundabout junction of main roads. It is named Cemmaes Road in reference to a former station which served the village of Cemmaes several miles to the north. No services are on offer here to walkers.

Looking down on Abercegir

Turn right at the Cemmaes Road roundabout to go down the verge beside A470 for 200 yards to the bridge over the Rover Dovey (Afon Dyfi), which is 9 miles from Machynlleth. Immediately over the bridge turn right on a track alongside the north bank of the river. After half a mile the track bends left to climb up towards a house. A footpath goes round left of it and climbs up, bending right as it does so. Go over a ridge and descend to pass another house. Briefly join the track of this house going north, then turn right on a path which climbs and bends around the northern side of Commins Gwalia. After passing Tynllwyn below your to the left turn right onto a road. After 150 yards going south on the road leave it at a bend on a track to the left. The track soon bends right to serve Bryn Moel but you carry on ahead eastwards on a path leading through after 400 yards to a road. Go left a short way then turn right on a track. After 100 yards the track climbs left but you go straight on along a path heading ENE along the south flank of Moel Eiddew. The path eventually climbs and enters the forest a mile from the road, where there is a seat.

Ignore the path going left and bend slightly right to a junction of tracks. Keep left and climb up for 300 yards. At the crossroads of paths and tracks just beyond the forest turn right to skirt the NE side of the forest. There is another seat just where you leave the forest and then descend steeply to an aerial mast. Follow the track down to the SE and turn left onto a footpath through Brynaire Farm. Bend right down and follow the path round to the left of another farm and join an access track to cross a bridge and turn left onto a road. Follow the road under the railway for access to the shop, pub and accommodation available in the village of Llanbrynmair, which is 15 miles from Machynlleth via Glyndwr's Way. Originally on the through route of Glyndwr's Way before the level crossing north of the village was closed, but now a short diversion, Llanbrynmair is a 19th century railway village, and consequently has no ancient buildings. However the station has been closed since 1965. A modest medieval church lies at Llan a mile and a half to the south, whilst half a mile to the west at Tafolwern is Domen Fawr, a motte and bailey castle built by Owain Cyfeiliog c1150 on a promontory between Afon Twymyn and Afon Rhiw Season.

Glyndwr's Way briefly joins the road heading north under the railway out of Llanbrynmair before turning right on a path going through a sequence of fields taking it nearly back to the railway. It then climbs up to the right of some woodland. After another 300 yards of climbing the bridleway goes left to avoid the farm of Cwm-carnedd and climbs to about 1100 feet. It then passes along the western side of the summit of the ridge of Cerrig y Tan, giving good views for over a mile before entering a forest. After a mile the bridleway crosses a forest track and continues heading NE for another three quarters of a mile before going out onto open land and bending round to the east, initially climbing but soon dropping down. After going through a gate keep right to follow a fence bending round to the left. The bridleway then drops more steeply. Eventually the way veers right and drops down to a bend of a road.

Go right along the road, passing a chapel at Neinthirion after half a mile and carrying on when a road comes in from the left. After another two thirds of a mile go left on a track to Dolwen and then right on another track. After half a mile go left at a junction of tracks to pass north of Moel Ddolwen. Go left at another junction of tracks and climb up to leave the obvious track and go right through a gate onto open and boggy moorland. A bridleway then heads NE along the south side of Pen Coed for almost a mile. Occasional posts help to indicate the way for almost a mile before the path keeps left of a house and heads north. Another house is passed and then the way goes left and climbs up round Bryn-derwen. The way then goes east to descend to a lane. The original route than followed the lane past the much restored 15th century church of St Cadfan to reach the A458 at Llangadfan, which is 26 miles from Machynlleth. If in a hurry to reach the Cann Office Hotel this is still the best option. Glyndwr's Way has a more convoluted route. It turns left off the lane after just 100 yards and crosses a boggy field and a new bridge to reach another lane, which is followed left for 70 yards before going down the farm track towards Bryneyrch. Pass left of the farm across a field and then go down a lane. Take a path to the right to cut through to another lane. When this bends round to head south use the footbridge on the left to cross the Afon Banwy to reach A458.

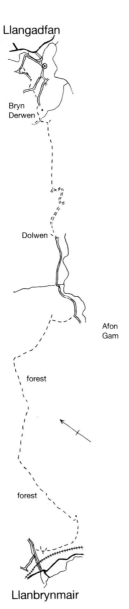

one mile

Llangadfan

Bryn
Derwen

Dolwen

Afon
Gam

forest

forest

Llanbrynmair

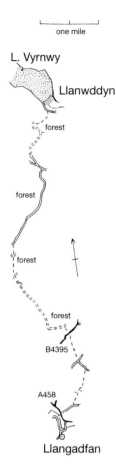

one mile

L. Vyrnwy

Llanwddyn

forest

forest

forest

forest

B4395

A458

Llangadfan

After crossing A458 at Llangadfan the Way heads NE on a lane for 200 yards. Fork left up the track towards Blowty for a few yards and then go through a new kissing gate on the right to go up through two fields bypassing the farm. Keep straight on a junction of paths. Go over a raise and through a gate and then in the large field keep to the fence on the left, descending to cross a stream and climb back up to a road. Go left on the road and at a T-junction go straight over onto a path heading NNW. Cross the valley of a stream and climb up to Penyfford. Cross over B4395 into the forest heading NW on a bridleway. After 100 yards go left onto a forest track. Carry along the track past the section where the right-hand side is open. Then go over two crossings of forest tracks. After 100 yards go left on a poorer track and descend to a track. Cross over it onto a track by a field which drops down to a ford and footbridge. Shortly afterwards join a tarmac head heading NE first with forest on both sides, then with views down to the right. After the bridge at Dol Cownwy go left then immediately right on a track towards Bryn Cownwy. Bear right before the house and climb steeply. The gradient eases after a crossing of tracks. After another 150 yards the track bends left to reach the forest edge. You will then get a view of the dam of Lake Vyrnwy. A path following a field edge then drops down to the road to the dam, which passes a craft centre, cafes, the entrance to a sculpture trail, and toilets with taps and sinks. Originally Glyndwr's Way followed the road crossing the dam, which is 32 miles from Machynlleth, and went down B4396.

The dam at Lake Vyrnwy

The straining tower at Lake Vyrnwy

Lake Vyrnwy is a reservoir supplying Liverpool via aqueducts 68 miles long Begun in 1881, the dam is 144ft high and 1170ft long, and was Britain's first large-scale masonry dam. It holds back 13 million gallons of water in a five mile long lake first filled in 1888. The road over the dam is carried on arches under which water cascades when the lake is full. The lake shores have been planted with conifers and form a nature reserve looked after by the R.S.P.B. By the northern shore a mile NW of the dam is a circular straining tower in the form of a castle complete with machicolations and copper spires on the main tower and its staircase turret. The tower is 200ft high but with the lower 50ft under water. The lake flooded the site of the village of Llanwddyn and its medieval church, necessitating the building of a new village of that name to the east.

From the dam retrace your steps past the craft centre and go straight ahead on a tarmac road. Just before Grwn-oer a gate leads off left to bypass the farm. Rejoin a track beyond it and go gently downhill for 500 yards. Turn left and cross a bridge over the River Vyrnwy, one mile from the dam. Look left to find a shop at a junction of B-roads, and still further round to the left are toilets with taps and sinks, however your route is to the right, heading SSE on B4393. After 500 yards at a hairpin bend of the main road turn right (effectively straight on) onto a minor road, passing a bus shelter. After 200 yards go through a gate on the left to find a path up through trees. After 500 yards the path will have descended again to a road. Go a few yards to the right, then take a track heading back to the left. After a short distance go through a gate on the right to ascend very steeply on a forest path. Go left when the path levels out at a track and go right at a junction of forest tracks after a short distance. After 300 yards there is a gate across the path as it descends to Pen-yr-allt and at that point you go right ascending steeply to start with on a path. The path levels out and crosses an open field with forest all around except below to the east. Go through a gate and descend steeply through forest and at the bottom turn right for 30 yards. Go right and descend a new set of wooden steps and then keep close to the wall to a stile. Carry on through woodland to a new gate onto an open field. Go across the field, keeping well to the left of the house. Go round the edge of woodland until a church is in view. Keep to the right, as although the church is your objective it is reached by joining a track behind caravans south of the church, and then heading north to reach it. The church is that of St Mary at Pont Llogel, built in 1854 at the expense of Sir Watkin Williams-Wynn.

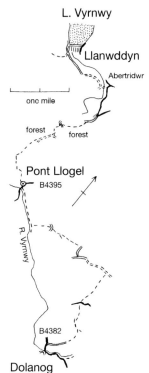

Sculpture Park at Llanwddyn

From Pont Llogel Church turn right to go south a few yards along B4395. Just before the bridge go left, passing a trail notice-board and picnic tables. For the next half mile the trail follows a track along the wooded north bank of the river, merging along this section with part of the route of a walk commemorating the hymn composer Anne Griffiths. An open field is crossed and then after a bridge over Nant Llwyd the ways diverge again and Glyndwr's Way climbs up to the left. Go straight on up the bridleway when a track comes in from the right. After 400 yards from the bridge the way crosses a road and goes down a track to Pentre. The bridleway goes along the south side of some woodland to reach a road, 500 yards beyond Pentre. Turn right to head south on the road, which descends to cross a stream and then steeply climbs back up again. At a junction turn left along a byway and gently climbs for half a mile. Turn right on a path which after a while drops down. Turn left along the track connecting Dolwar Fach to B4382. Go right down the road a few yards and then through a gate onto a path ascending the north flank of Allt Dolanog keeping at right-angles to the road. Go to the right of a hump and bend slightly left then right to go over the ridge between humps. The path passes a small old quarry and woods on the right before descending steeply. Turn right onto a byway and continue to drop gently down into the village of Dolanog, 41 miles from Machynlleth. You will pass toilets with sinks and taps on the left, and then a shop after turning left onto B4382 to cross the River Vyrnwy. Do not be tempted to use a short-cut lane avoiding the main road since it rejoins the main road only by means of a ford and a broken-down bridge which is now closed.

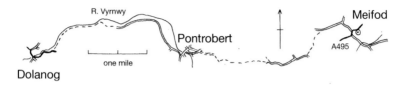

Meifod

R. Vyrnwy

Pontrobert

A495

one mile

Dolanog

From Dolanog follow B4382 for 400 yards. A short while after the road leaves the river bank a path on the left takes you back to the river bank. In trees for much of the way, the path is perched high above the south side of the river for the next mile before climbing away from it to reach a track which runs parallel to the river for another mile and a half to Pontrobert. Turn left and just before crossing the bridge you will find on the right a small piece of open land with tables and seats, wood sculptures, and a small shop close at hand.

Having crossed Pontrobert bridge, which lies 44 miles from Machynlleth, keep right, following the road along the river bank. After 100 yards fork left to climb up to a diamond crossing of roads. Go right, heading east on a dead-end road, from which leads a path across two fields to a track down to Dolobran Hall. Go a few yards to the right towards the farm and then go through a gate into a field. Keep right and follow the field boundary, which beyond a corner is beside a belt of trees. Continue heading east beyond the trees, crossing the valley of a small stream. Climb back up and pass to the left of Coed-cowrhyd to join the track connecting it with a lane. Turn right down the lane, keeping straight on to head ENE at a junction of lanes. After 130 yards the road bends right to pass round the hill of Gallt yr Dyffryn but you go left through a gate onto a path passing round the left or NW flank of the hill. The path becomes a woodland track through to a lane. Turn right for 250 yards and then at Pentre (which has a campsite) go right on a wider road to reach A495 as it runs through the village of Meifod, which is 47miles from Machynlleth and has a pub and shop.

Cross-slab, Meifod Church

The church of St Tysilio and St Mary at Meifod is the most interesting of the old churches along the route of Glyndwr's Way. It is attractively located in a large churchyard with some tall trees which once contained three churches. This was a clas or Celtic monastic settlement from which churches at Alberbury, Guilsfield, Llanfair Caereinion and Welshpool were founded and was a burial place of the princes of Powys, one of whom is commemorated by a very fine cross-slab inside. The church has remnants of a fully aisled 12th century nave, a rare survival in Wales, and was probably then cruciform with a pair of transepts. The south transept has been swallowed up into a wide aisle built in the 14th century alongside the original chancel. The north aisle matching it is Victorian. One and half arches survive of the 12th century arcades, that on the north open towards a vestry, and that on the south now blocked up and part of an outside wall. The tower is 15th century but the tower arch towards the nave has responds which appear to be reset 12th century work. Old furnishings include a 16th century font, a Jacobean pulpit and 17th century altar rails.

Go a short distance down A495 at Meifod heading south and then go right on the minor road to cross the River Vyrnwy on a bridge of 1865. After 100 yards beyond the bridge turn left onto a narrow lane which climbs above the river Turn right onto a path after 400 yards and climb, steeply at first, on a path which levels out to give good views of the river. Carry on up through trees and on reaching a field keep to its right-hand boundary. Llyn Du now appears in view on the right. Keep heading east, passing left of a belt of trees to reach a road. Turn right and enjoy the even better views of the lake. Go straight on at a crossroads. After three quarters of a mile the road bends left. Fork right and descend for 150 yards to find a path going back to the left. Drop down to a stream and climb back up to where there is a derelict timber-framed cottage partly covered in corrugated iron sheeting. Go right through a gate and follow the left-hand field boundary. The path climbs to pass round the left (east) side of a house. Cross over a road into a large field and aim for the right-hand side of a belt of woodland. Turn left onto a road which descends for 150 yards before you turn left to drop steeply on a path to cross a stream. Climb gently back up and pass left of a house and go through to the farm of Pant, beyond which is a caravan site. Keep right of the farm to join its lane by a tiny pool and carry on up to the B4392.

Turn right for 120 yards along B4392 and then go left onto a lane for 500 yards. Go over a stile into a field and keep above the track down to the farm until the last moment. Keep left of the farm on a track, and then go left over a stream to go through a gate into a field and turn right. This leads through to a path through newly planted woodland. After 150 yards ignore the wide track ahead and climb very steeply on a rough path up through trees. Cross over a track and keep climbing more gently. The path bears slightly right to descend the other side. After a while it levels out and goes through woods. Turn right

for 100 yards then go through a gate to cross over a field (newly ploughed at the time of writing). The path bends left and descends to cross a stream. Keep close to the left of a fence as you climb back up to a road. Go right a few yards then left into a field, keeping fairly close to the road as far as a small quarry, after which bear left. The path goes round the left-hand side of a hump and crosses a stream on a new bridge. Climb up to a track and head right a short distance, then go left to climb up steeply on a rough track. This brings you up onto the northern side of Y Golfa and keeps you off the golf course south of the path. After 300 yards of level path a final short steep climb takes you up to the triangulation point, giving a wonderful panorama.

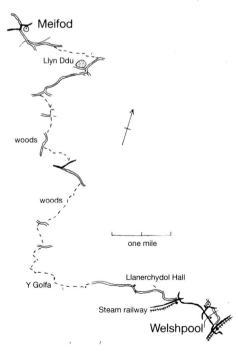

Narrow guage steam train near Welshpool

From the triangulation point on the summit of Y Golfa the path descends due east and passes through the edge of woodland and down to pass left of a conspicuous white farm house. It then joins a track which passes a barn and heads east. It becomes a gently descending tarmac estate road through the parkland of Llanerchydol Hall, which can be glimpsed if you look back left further down. Much of the hall was built for David Pugh and is dated 1820, but the west wing is of c1870 and there is an older core. The last part of the estate road lies above the terminal station of the Welshpool and Llanfair Light Railway, a 2ft 6inch gauge line opened in 1903. It carried freight only from 1931 until it closed in 1956, only to be re-opened by enthusiasts in 1963. There are three trains each way at weekends from Easter onwards, Tuesday to Thursday as well in June and July and every day in August.

The estate road makes a last minute wiggle left and right and joins A490. Go left and immediately arrive at a roundabout junction of main roads. Cross over, passing the entrance to Raven Square station of the steam railway and head east down into Welshpool (Y Trallwng). The turretted tower visible on the right on the way in belongs to Christchurch, built in 1839-44 and you will pass a number of 16th and 17th houses interspersed with later buildings. Carry on down the main street of the town, going over the main crossroads past the town hall. Cross over the canal and immediately turn left into a small canal-side garden to find a notice board and a stone marking the termination of Glyndwr's Way, 58 miles from Machynlleth. From the garden there is direct access onto the canal tow-path forming the Severn Way, which if followed for two miles northwards leads to a junction with Offa's Dyke path which offers a walking route southwards back down to your starting point at Knighton. To reach Welshpool station from the garden carry on further SE down the main road for 150 yards to a roundabout and go straight on beyond it. There is a motte and bailey castle site 120yards north of the station.

Road leading into Welshpool

Welshpool is a busy town of about 7000 people and was once the county town of Montgomeryshire. It offers the full range of shops, accommodation and other services that backpackers and walkers might require. There are several things of interest around the town, which became known in England as Welshpool to distinguish it from the town of Poole in Dorset. Down by a lock on the canal is the Powisland Museum. Further north lies a very rare survival, an octagonal cockpit of brick, originally an adjunct of the Castle Inn, where cockfights were staged until they were made illegal in 1849. To the east lies the parish church of St Mary or St Cynfelyn. It has an irregular layout with a 13th century west tower and a mid 14th century chancel out of axis with each other. In the 16th century a central nave with north and south aisles was laid out to replace an older layout with two naves of similar width. The 14th century south porch was swallowed into the side of the south aisle. In the 18th century the tower was heightened and both aisles rebuilt. They now have Victorian windows. Beyond and below the church is the house of Grace Evans, reputed to have been given to her as a reward for her part in the subterfuge that enabled Lady Nithsdale to smuggle her husband out of the Tower of London, where he was awaiting execution for his part in the 1715 Jacobite rebellion.

Grace Evans' house in Welshpool

The cockpit at Welshpool

Stone at the end of the trail by the canal in Welshpool

In a park SW of Welshpool between Glyndwr's Way and the Severn Way following the Shropshire Union Canal lies Powis Castle, a splendid National Trust property. Once known to the Welsh as Castell Coch, and close to an older motte, it is a sandstone building on an elevated site begun in c1280 by Gruffydd ap Gwenwynwyn, Prince of Powys. His son Owain took the English type surname de la Pole and left a daughter who married John de Charlton. Here in 1403 Edward, 5th Lord Charlton was blockaded by his own tenants in support of Owain Glyndwr. Subsequently the castle was divided between the Greys and the Suttons, and later held by the Herberts, created lords Powis, who remodelled the castle as a stately home with fine terraced gardens. In 1644 Parliamentary forces captured the castle in a surprise night attack.

DEFINITIONS USED IN THE ROUTE DESCRIPTIONS

Bridleway - Right of way for walkers and riders. Signed as for paths.
                        Not necessarily marked on the ground when crossing fields.
Farm Lane - A dead end road leading just to one or two farms or houses.
Forest   - Planted conifers, mostly too densely set to walk between.
Green Lane - A grass-covered track with a hedge or fence on both sides.
Lane   - A little used tarmac road mostly the width of one vehicle only.
Path   - Right of way on foot only. Signed by occasional badges at gates.
                        Not always marked on the ground when crossing a field..
Road   - Tarmac surface mostly wide enough for cars to pass each other.
Saddle   - A lower gap between two summits on a ridge.
Track   - Clearly marked way with gravel or dirt surface of cart width.
                        A feint track has same width but more of a green surface.
Woods   - Natural deciduous trees, and/or conifers not densely planted.

Turn off means at about 90 degrees. Fork off means at 45 degrees or less.
Bridges used to take paths and bridleways over marshland or streams can be
anything from a board or two planks to structures with steps and handrails.

ENVIRONMENTAL IMPACT

Basically; Leave nothing but footprints, take away nothing but photographs.
Don't leave any litter and be very discrete when wild camping (see page 5)
Don't make a lot of noise when passing close farms and houses.
Don't stray from the path on sections where you can clearly see where it goes
Don't touch farming or forestry equipment. Leave all gates as you find them.

FURTHER READING

Abbeys, Priories & Cathedrals of Wales, Mike Salter, 2012.
The Castles of Mid Wales, Mike Salter, 2nd edition 2001.
The Old Parish Churches of Mid Wales, Mike Salter, 2nd edition 2003.
Powys (Buildings of Wales series) Richard Haslam, 1979.
Other guides to Glyndwr's Way exist but are now likely to be very out of date.

NAVIGATIONAL AIDS

The route described in this book from Knighton to Welshpool crosses the Ordnance Survey Landranger Maps numbers 137, 136, 136, 125 and 126. The trail
is mostly fairly well signed but there are some high moorland sections where
you could easily wander off it in poor visibility. Always carry a map and com-
pass and know how to use them. A useful item is a Global Positioning System.
You can check your speed and distance, and time travelled, but best of all it
will give you grid references accurate to a few feet. It can also be used to find
geocaches but currently there are few of these on or near Glyndwr's Way.

OUTDOOR SAFETY

Boots and proper outdoor clothing and waterproofs are essential for this walk,
much of which is on rough surfaces above the 300 metre contour. Sort out any
problems with feet, footwear or socks immediately. Carry enough clothes to
remain warm even in the most wet and stormy conditions and have enough
food and drink so that you don't have to rush unduly or take risks. Only very
fast walkers will cover much more than two miles an hour on this trail even if fit,
lightly loaded and ground and weather conditions are favourable.

USEFUL WEBSITES AND OTHER INFORMATION

www.backpackersclub.co.uk - Club supporting backpacking in the UK.
www.geocaching.com   - Finding caches using a GPS system.
www.idwa.org.uk   - The Long Distance Walkers Association.
www.nationaltrail.co.uk   - Details of long-distances walks in the UK
www.thetrainline.com   - Rail times, connections and various fares.

National Rail Enquiries: 08457 48 49, 50   Buses: Traveline: 0870 608 2 608
Glyndwr's Way Trail Officer: gwnt@powys.gov.uk   01597 827562
Tourist Information Offices: Knighton, Llanidloes, Machynlleth, Welshpool.

Several holiday companies offer baggage handling from point to point along
the trail, allowing you to walk each day with just what you require for that day.

The southern approach to Machynlleth along Glyndwr's Way